Discipline

You look at me with hurt, defiant eyes.
Rebellious child, how can I say
That I, once swearing elders all unwise,
Vowed not to rule as they?

Your chin out-thrust, obedient you turn
To hide your angry sobs.   If years
Should make of you a parent, you may learn,
These tyrants, too, shed tears.

For those who have loved the singer —
and expected her to sing her best...

TYRANT'S TEARS
A COLLECTION OF POEMS

BY
BETTY COOK ROTTMANN

Sheba Review, Incorporated • Jefferson City, Missouri • USA

CONTENTS

CRY FROM THE PARAPET...

PEACE WALKERS

Churchboards, prayer wheels, nuns' beads,
For someone's good intentions...

If I had faith in prayer
To more than deepen one's own sensitivities,
Then I would pray
For walkers seeking peace.

And caution them: "Beware of ghosts
Along the route of your parade—
Ghosts of the innocents;
The brave who stopped some madness;
The ghosts of still more innocents
If maddened men sweep after far retreating lines.
All ample are the ghosts
Of women who have wept from history's parapets
To watch their men in combat on the plain..."

I would pray
The walkers are not duped again
Within, without, so taunted to confront
Those saying, "Young are foolish to have faith
In principles they have been taught."

A FABLE FOR AMERICAN MOTHERS

There was once a good mother.
She took her children to church each Sunday.
Scolded them when they quarreled or destroyed things,
Loved them dearly, and made them cookies once a week.

One day the government sent her son to a far country.

When he wrote:
    Today a small boy tripped a mine
    Intended for our tank, and he was blown to bits.
    How can I sleep tonight?
She cried a little, and wrote back:
    Did you get your cookies this week?

When he wrote:
    We flattened villages and rows of ancient rubber trees
    To reveal the enemy,
    And are guarding the villagers in their new sandbagged
    compound
    But the sad eyes waiting for their dole of rice keep
    haunting me.
She cried a little more, and then wrote back:
    Do you like the soft cookies or the chewy ones better?

When he wrote:
    I am torn apart by conscience and allegiance.
    Why won't anyone do something there
    Before these people and their countryside
    And we, along with them, are all destroyed?
The mother cried a long time over this, and then wrote back:
    You forgot to tell me whether I should send
    The ones with raisins in them, or with coconut...

CLEARING THE BO LOI WOODS

He watched the Rome plows furrow through
Tall rubber trees, bulldozers massing grotesque heaps
As crews were making it a game.

The order on his clipboard read
That these nine thousand acres cleared
Would leave the enemy exposed.

Impassive, sandalled peasants, pausing on the road
To shift their burdens, gave no sign,
Except for one young woman with a boy
Who skipped beside her, stick in hand.
Her look was long and straight upon
The desolation and the officer in green.

(Quite suddenly
He saw himself a boy again, with axe in hand,
Caught in the forest by his mother, eyes ablaze
At wanton waste of trees...and life...)

He turned his back to peasants, child and Bo Loi Woods,
Striking his fist against the order board
In shame.

VIGIL

Deep up the nave of night
Stars flicker in galactic winds.
They give no solace...
Votive lights, their burning ineffectual
On altars of the vast Immutable.

These are but planets, orbiting,
Ablaze or frozen,   or—if like our own—
Where, underneath still other stars,
Men creatures crouch in battle fear
As their own lethal comets streak the sky,
While mothers grieve upon far windowsills
And young wives, tearful, bend above
Their sleeping children who may well be fatherless
Before another night is lit by stars.

BEREAVED

She walked
Erect, aloof
Intensely wide of eye
Within the parched expanse of days
That rimmed the desert of her early grief,
While those who loved her prayed to see
One rain of tears to ease
Her forlorn, arid heart.

FERN FORETELLING

Our garden ferns lie brittle-gray
Beneath white drifting snow
Of year-end holy days.

Brought gently from low sheltered banks
Of our home stream, these ferns' rich summer
Greenness held remembrances — of countrysides
In this and other climes — long shared
With family and friends.

These withered fronds cannot survive snow winterkill.
But curled below, fern hearts
Lie ready to uncoil new fronds — some power bids them grow.

Alike, some power underlying cold
Of war and hate, bids men and women here, afar,
Bind time with knowledge into force,
Uncoiling one day into greening spring of peace.

HER POINT OF VIEW...

EVE'S CHOICE

When verdant boughs
Hung every path with fruit
As beautiful, as tart or sweet...
Why this and only this?

Because a woman must ask why.

Why not?

NEW NAMING OF WOMEN

For centuries
Unnumbered, women have been named
As mothers, daughters, sisters, wives,
Less beautiful, unmarried...always by
Relationship or in comparison
With someone else.

Let us have done with it.

Come, trek with me
Through dictionary, thesaurus, through
Linguistic wilderness yet unexplored,
In search of words to name us well—
Unrelative and singular,
INCOMP'RABLE!

MASQUERADE

She's chosen the gowns and the masks she'll wear—
Fey, coquettish, or free—
For a role she assumes will be different, fair.
No one will know it is she.

As seasons fall past, features slowly align—
Subtly the molding is done.
Comes the day, she will look for herself but to find
Mask and the masker are one.

SUNDAY SERVICE

For this she has ironed many ruffles smooth
And supervised the polishing of shoes.
Allowed the clock to call out one more day
That little sleepyheads must wake and dress...
To bring her children to this quiet place,
To sit here with her husband's hand in hers.

Into the simple sanctuary now
Soft-filtered sunlight flows, on past the head
Of Shepherd, and of lamb, to touch upon
Each small blond head beside her in the pew.

Full organ waves swell softly and then fall
Against a bank of glowing altar flowers,
As from a rustling page a voice reads low:
"By waters cool doth He restore my soul."

Now this one Sunday hour becomes for her
A holy, still and shining pool, to which
Her heart will come to drink again and yet
Again, all through the hurried week ahead.

FUNERAL GIFTS

"What a devoted daughter you have been,"
The neighbors said as they brought in
Their pies and covered casseroles.

"How nice that you stayed home to care for him
These twenty years." She laughed her little laugh
And set the dishes out in rows as neat
As all the other things about the house.

Still others came with plants and anecdotes...
In tribute to the man they all had known,
But she had made her offering—intangible—
Long years ago, and so had nothing more to give.

TEA WITH PORTENT

I lean against the door of this new day,
A morning cup of tea in hand, heart gay
With sense of Juneness.   I would imitate
My neighbor wren—exultant, sing away
Before my nest, a-tremor with the pride
Of young ones still cocooned by sleep inside,
And pleasure from a husband's parting kiss—
For thought, portentous, suddenly has cried

To drink this blend of summer fullness deep,
To savor well its taste, as if to keep
It for a charm against another day
That could arouse me from contented sleep,

Confronted with the stark necessity
To share my morning cup with tragedy.

TREE HOUSE

She found it in an apple tree—
A blossom-fragrant bower
Transformed by childish imagery
Into Rapunzel's tower.

A secret refuge, from which height
Grim parents were not tall.
There, sifted through the dappled light,
Her troubles, too, grew small.

Throughout her womanhood she came
In spirit to renew
Perspective. Something that she called
Her "tree-house point of view."

TABLE TALK

For this her mother taught her how to say
Her words as clearly as a small child could.
For this she read her childhood nights away
And filled herself with literary food;
Engaged in hours of student repartee
And matched her wits with all who would—
In confidence that, with her learning done,
She could converse at length with anyone.

For this? To huddle in an acrid haze
Hemmed in by trumpets' cacaphonous cries
Half-drowning bibulous clichés
That ridicule intelligent replies?

Denied her wit and well-turned phrase,
She masks frustration with averted eyes
And steeps her words in gin. Why not? It's clear
An intellect is most unwelcome here.

REGARDING WAYS OF LOVING...

LOVE SONG IN TWO VERSIONS

The very young are tuning up their hearts
For music in this loveliest of springs,
Although uncertain where the music starts
Or what cadenzas each new rapture brings.

For older loves, their sum of springs imparts
Some mastery. The young untutored things,
All novices, pursue mere melodies;
The old, as artists, create symphonies.

NOSTALGIA

Each year when lilac-laden spring comes round
And gives my old romantic heart a turn,
I long to be a sorceress, one bound
On brewing up love potions. In some urn
I'd crush the lilacs, purple, white and blue
And, blending in the scent of budding pine,
Dissolve them all in moonlight mixed with dew.
Then stealthily dispense this brew of mine
Alike upon the puritan, the staid,
The hearts abandoned or betrayed, the shy—
And equally, for every man and maid.

Oh, well I know the world must work. But I
Recall as well how bittersweet the sting
Of being young—and lonely—in the spring.

PROGRESSION

I thought my love for you began in spring—
A mere presentiment by April moon—
And even with our summer vows and ring
Came intimation, but not love so soon.

Love came instead by wintertime—of year
And stricken heart. Beside your bed of white
I watched, bound there by a new fear
Each day of vigil lost in weeping night.

That journey into pain you made alone.
And as you lay there, bravely, silently,
Your pleading eyes were seeking out my own.
Because it was a world unknown to me,
I could but hold your hand across the gloom—
I learned to love you in that quiet room.

DIRECTION

How can a mentor be content to teach
A child to earn his keep, no more?   For he
Still would be poor with no means in his reach
To temper life through creativity:
To sob despair into a song; tame rage
In strokes upon a canvas; measure strife
By forceful words upon a written page;
And—with a mind fed well on books—when life
Grips, and the knot of strain pulls taut,
Withdraw to quiet corridors of thought.

SECOND MARRIAGE

Guests find no candles or white satin here —
Only some shadowed ghosts of younger hopes
Long dwindled, now revived again.

Thin lines around her tense mouth show
Just segments of her story, known too well,
Her sense of desperation, and new fright.
This time, she prays, this time, love must win out.
Hearing his promise for the future with one ear,
She finds the other throbs with echoes of the past...the past.

It was most wise to keep her wedding small
With such a crowd of ghosts about.

THE GAME

When she was small it was an easy task
To snatch her up from hazard,
Hold her close and safe within my arms.
Sometimes she sobbed to be denied
The pretty danger, or from hurt
Of my quick, silent grasp.

Now, there are words to warn and parallels
To draw and odds to figure.   Comes a time
I must no longer snatch her up or stop the game,
But stand aside with inward agony
To watch her test the laws of chance,
And often lose.

FOREST PAIR

Two hemlocks rise beside
Each other in the darkened green,
Their pungent boughs, their crusted bark
Alike and not alike.

Some branches of the Old
Are dying now; the Younger still
Outreaching toward maturity;
Yet neither one will lean.

They stand apart, though roots
Commingle deep, unseen,
Within the black earthmold that holds
All long-dead hemlock pairs.

Their boughs, though close and blown
By selfsame winds, brush against
Each other only now and then
In self-restraint, yet lovingly.

A SON, AGED TWENTY-ONE

Twice must I bear this son. Though first pangs brought
Him to my arms, those next must send him on
Into the world. This second time for me
No anesthesia, no clean cut of knife,
No surgeon's twist of severed cord. My son,
In angry haste for manhood, strains away
With independence I have nurtured well
From first shoelaces through first love. Despite
All good advice, I am as unprepared
For this as for my first travail with him.

Yet, I must spread my arms and set him free.
Though yearning, bear this birth with dignity.

IN MEMORY

You have gone, my companion true,
But earth's beauty you taught me to see
Still surrounds. So I walk alone
Lush green pathways we made our own.
Reveling in their richness will be
My own best memorial to you.

FULFILLMENT

I knew, dear Joseph, it would be a Son.
The angel promised me. So fair a One
Will wear the royal purple well. For now
Just wrap Him in the cloth my cousin spun.

And now the sound of singing comes again!
How could I hear a choir—it is the strain
Of our long trip, the birth. Did I presume
A Holy Child would not be borne in pain?

Please tell the shepherds at the door our plight.
They surely would not cast out into night
Our little lamb, safe in their manger here.
We have no lantern, and yet all is light...

Why do the shadows of the rafters fall
So like a cross against our stable wall?

APPRAISAL

Miss Six-Years-Old, I see you preening there
Before the mirror in your Sunday clothes.
It tells you truthfully that you are fair.
It will continue truthful as you pose
In years ahead—when, radiant as a rose,
You ask if you're in love.   Heartbreak, alas,
You won't conceal with freshly-powdered nose.

Gray hair will show, and lines, as seasons pass—
No one will be as honest as your looking-glass.

ANOTHER VIEW...

HIGH SCHOOL LESSON

Miss Brown, as I recall, was wan and thin,
With clothes that did not fit. Her jutting chin
Thrust out, she scratched upon the board
A daily verse culled from some treasure-hoard.

Although the courses that she tried to teach
Continued somehow to elude my reach,
In retrospect, it seems but fair to tell—
The truths her verses taught have served me well.

BIRD SONG

The day the cat crept throught the hedge—
Left crushed blue shells and ravelled wild
Nest-weavings where the songbird lives—
I scarcely had consoled my child
When overhead the bird, on wing,
Began its roundelay. "How can it sing?"

Discovery drew her damp eyes wide.
"The song is all that's left," she cried.

MOUNTAIN CABIN VISITOR

They scarcely had arrived before
She was at work—breaking away
Dead branches near the eaves,
Sweeping pine needles from the path.

Returning with the wood, he set
The broom aside, and gently led
Her deep into the trees, still murmuring
That she was only making order. "Yes,
You were. But here we are the guests
In Nature's house, who, in her ordering
Encompasses the barren, old and dead..."

ABSTRACTING APPLE PIE

Each time I ask for apple pie,
You smile.
Now do you think I only long
For nutmeg-fragrant morsels
In a wedge of crust?

I'm really leaning out my window
To let apple-blossom snow come feathering
Down upon my head, light into my hands...
I'm polishing red roundness on my jeans
To bite into, while peering down
At those who walk unknowingly beneath my tree...

I'm lying in the rusting grass,
My basket still half-filled, while I
Have stopped to savor ripeness
In the fruit and in my life...
Even an apple pie is so much more.

LITERARY HOUR

The young professor, quietly intent,
Spread out upon the stand
Her sheaf of verse to plead its cause.

And, having read from Dickinson to Angelou,
She acquiesced to creaking chairs
And rested poetry's case.

None missed the two or three who quickly left—
Foregoing coffee in the paper cups
And talk with petit-fours in hand—
To set some lines on paper just once more
And brood upon them half the night.

STAR LINKS

Tall locusts rise against this holiday's cascading scrim
Of white. Their branches sigh, ice-weary in the cold,
Commingling with faint stars pulled close
By skills stretching an unknown universe,
While making smaller still this world we know.

Those swifter stars — the satellites — cast webs
Invisibly across our separate lands
To link all into commonalities
Of hunger, pain and deep desire.

Newly aware, we are compelled to pull
From our diverse beliefs the husks —
Long nurtured — of old fears and hates,
Discovering, within, those mutual cores
That plead for love and peace.

AUTOMATION

Knowing death waited somewhere in the deck,
She programmed her life—to the parameters
Its format would allow—with Laughter squared
And Love to the nth power.

IN DUE SEASON...

POSSESSIONS

Look long upon all loveliness
Make note of every melody;
Touch satin, stone, and revel
In each fragrance, and each pungency...

No matter what you have in hand,
All you have known
You own.

FAIR WARNING

Beware the Ides of March.   Conniving Spring,
With little boys and kites, comes luring men
To race with her against the wind, to fling
Themselves upon some greening hillside.   Then
Each kite-tug pulls into remembering
Old kites and springs that will not come again...

Beware of March, unless you can defy
The heartache in a kite against the sky.

RED MAPLE IN WINTER

She shivered in her dark chemise,
Divested of her gypsy glow
By Winter.   Then, relenting, he
Tossed over her a cape of snow.

LONGING

She comes a moment to the farmhouse door
And, pausing, wipes her hands upon her dress.
Beyond the sagging fence, her eyes caress
New-tasseled corn, black-purple at its core,
And, off the lane, green seas of rye.   Before
A whispering summer-scented wind, they press
Themselves in wave on wave of restlessness
Against a bank of towering sycamores.

She wanders through the yard, bare as in drought,
Where gray weeds find their way through rusting rims
While hens scratch through the dust in draggled state,
She sighs for summer greenness there fenced out;
Then fills a battered pail until it brims
And waters one wild rosebush at the gate.

MAIDENS

Gaudy Autumn, wayward strumpet,
Gaily beckons men to follow
As she flaunts her gypsy colors,
Feigning flight through hill and hollow.

Buxom Summer meets her lovers
In green fields, her gold hair blowing;
Even Spring, shy lassie, flutters
Pastel lashes, blushes glowing.

Only Winter shrouds her beauty
With a gray-on-gray creation
Few are those who—color sated—
Sense her muted revelation.

DISCOVERY

I never knew the solace of the sea
Before, but having found it, I have fed
Repeatedly upon its memory
Of warming sand, the scent of fish long dead
Yet mingled with new life; of tension shed
While watching endless waves beat endless shore
To make an endlessness of time ahead...

I fling myself beside the muffled roar
Again in flight, and with white sea gulls soar.

CYCLE

In childhood it was my delight
To scamper through dry leaves, piled bright
In crumpled gold and scarlet haze
Along October's woodland ways.

Now I am grown and those there be
Who frown on such frivolity.

So, when October brings the yen
To scuffle in dry leaves again,
I camouflage my bent for fun
And take along my little son.

AUTUMN CHOREOGRAPHY

October has her mischief done: the leaves are gypsies. Every one
Sheds summer green for dancing gown of amber, gold or russet brown.
Whirling, they flee, intent to find romance in czardas with the wind.
When their gyrations make them tire, old gardeners rake them for a fire.

A glowing, gallant way to die — one mad last pirouette to sky!

REJUVENATION

Spring again...it must be so—
The jonquils knew it days ago.
Young frogs rehearse beside their pond
With greening meadows just beyond.

Fair, fragrant earth now seems to be
Waking, in hushed expectancy.
My love and I link hands again
To reminisce along the lane

And stroll unmindful of the years
Elapsed in struggle, or the tears
So vainly shed...only aware
That Spring and Love are everywhere.

What matters time? To this we hold,
Though aging, we do not grow old
As long as each new, pulsing Spring
Can stir our hearts to wakening.

THE WATCHERS

The night and I are old and silent friends
Who long have kept dark watch above a world
That sleeps, while from the hills that round us in
With moonlit-patterned leaves, a pendant time
Sifts out slow hours, unmarked by shadowed clocks.

With intimate communion, first we sense
The softest murmur of a restless bird
Or shuffing of pine tangled wind.   And then
A pause...still, all so still, that breathing comes
As an affront, till quietness is past.

Who never keeps a watch with night could miss
An interval of immortality.

FROM A HOSPITAL CORRIDOR...

REQUIEM FOR A LAME PRINCESS

At last
Her lithesome heart
That longed for beauty so
Slips from its shabby chrysallis
And formless, fair—
A-gossamer
May go.

DEPENDENT

Outside your quiet room gray winter rain
Keeps weeping vigil as you lie again
Among the gleaming maze devised to hold
You here, though in a white-spread world of pain.

Your heart, whose faint throb lifts the spread,
Declined to bow to bitterness, instead
Refined into a patient courage. I am shamed
Because I suffer less, yet am less kind.

But I am strong, and promise, as you start
On this new road of trial, to play my part.
Lean heavily upon my strength, for I
In turn must lean upon your valiant heart.

NEXT OF KIN

Around the waiting room in close-set rows
They face each other, and each wears
The sign of his own suffering. The men
Who have convinced themselves that they
Should never weep, now with taut jaws attempt
Some consolation for their sobbing wives.

Bewildered children, for whom the distraught
Can find no satisfying answer, droop
Or tease, or tug their mothers' skirts.

Here who can say which grief is more intense—
That of the old who know they soon must lose
The sharers of past dreams, or of the young
Whose future dreams lie dying down the hall?

HEAD NURSE

Sharp-tongued priestess, sweeping proudly
Through corridors in vestal white,
As if given charge by ancient gods
With some temple rite.

Scattering shy aides like frightened birds;
Overwhelming tearful families;
Keeping nurses ever vigilant
In their ministries.

Only when they fail will she appear
Where the anguished patient lies—
Deft her hands, then, sure and comforting,
Gentle, too, her eyes.

SICK CHILD

A mother has so little time to weep,
For smiling, constant vigil she must keep
Beside the white bed, helpless to explain
To one so small the mystery of pain—
Aware that with her own first tear will rise
A torrent from two apprehensive eyes.

Yet, when with crisis past and respite come,
She hurries to the ones she left at home
She will find clothes to wash and floors to sweep—
A mother has so little time to weep.

PANCHO ON THE RUN

Down the long corridor she trails the aide.
"Here is his room. You see, he has a view."

> — a fragile tree encircled by a bit of grass
> between his window and the room across the way
> and that a mirror image of his own, with bed
> and sagging man tied in his chair.

"Hello, dear girl!" He smiles
And pulls her closer with his trembling hand.
"Well now, tonight we've got old Pancho on the run.
How bright the moon shines on the desert hills!"

> — should she contest his statement,
> with the sunlight streaking on the wall?

He leans away. "It's good to see you but I have to go...
The Gen'ral's horse is restless. That's a dogrobber's* life."
He shuts his eyes and gallops back
Into the soldiering of his youth.

> — you see, he has a view.

* WWI term for officer's orderly

MOURNING

They smoothed your sheets and closed the drapes,
Then called me in for my goodbye.
Tearless, I touched your cooling hand.
   (My heart crept, moaning, out the door.)

They knelt beside my chair with opiates,
And asked their chaplain to come in.
Tearless, I thanked them and declined.
   (My heart ran, weeping, down the hall.)

I called our children and made plans
To rightly celebrate your life.
Tearless, I greeted all who came.
   (My heart fled, sobbing, to the woods.)

Now every closure has been signed,
my work resumed and friends renewed...

But, when alone within our room,
Dark witness to the love we shared,
Tearful at last, I join my heart
   To wander, wailing, through the nights.

SOLACE

Still grieving, one has need to go
Back to the pungent earth, to sow
More seed, to prune a vine or two...
Testing the faith one thought one knew.

IN LIGHTER VEIN...

ALL THE WRONG COURSES

Although her wall proudly displayed her degree,
She apparently studied in vain —
As she did none too well with the dragon she made
For her teenager's role in the autumn parade;
And she then disappointed her daughter of three
By thoughtlessly letting it rain.

VACATION ONSLAUGHT

Quick, stow the hose and hide the saw —
Aunt Emma called to say
The seasonal swarm of little boys
Is headed out our way.

Behind them, miles of trampled lawns,
Uprooted plants, and such;
For only the treasures best concealed
Escape their lethal touch.

No summer storm or hurricane
Exceeds in any way
The range of wide devastation wrought
By nephews come to stay.

IN THE PUBLIC DOMAIN

The Library is called an institution of public service,
A definition constantly broadened.

...A snug vestibule
    in which to wait for buses.
...A warm corner
    where old pensioners take afternoon naps.
...A row of tables
    at which teenagers lounge while watching for dates.
...A children's room
    where harried mothers leave scamps for hours.
...A desk with pen
    appropriated for last-minute themes and hasty lovenotes.
...An alcove
    where parcels are left while housewives are paying bills.
...A phone nook
    in which appointments and dates are made and broken.
...A drinking fountain
    where juveniles invite water fights.
...And
...Obscure sections of book stacks
    well-suited to a clandestine kiss...or two.

The Public Library also has books
to lend.

SIGNS OF A SEASON

Young robins sing gaily again from the elms;
Green wings on the maple shape news;
While gardeners busily sort out their bulbs,
Romance sorts young people by twos.

TRANSITION

Always before, my dream had been
Godlike and tall, an ideal sum
Of gallant princes found within
Far fairylands. And now you come
Only so tall, no charger, lance,
But with a strange, compelling glance—

I throw my storybooks aside
To spread love's primer pages wide.

MERCURY SKATING

Skimming along dingy walks, circling round,
Sped on new silvery wheels,
Little One, as if by magic, has found
Wings at her heels.

Feeling swift rushing of wind in her face,
Singing with newfound delight,
Little One flings small arms wide into space—
Skating is flight!

ALTERNATIVE

I find the pathway hard to choose
Between the heart and mind,
When heart bemoans head's lack of love
And head swears love is blind.

What if my heart, impetuous,
Ignores my reasoning head,
Then rues its choice, to learn that love
Needs also daily bread?

Should head hold sway, what bitter gain —
Leaving my heart behind,
Broken against restraining bars
Built by my clever mind?

WOMEN IN GRIEF

For many years I have been watching you.
At first in morning papers, now
By satellite and video —
Black-shawled, black-veiled and wailing, arms
Cradling your dead, or flung imploringly
At sky, in funeral lines
To destinations off the page or television screen.

You were remote,
Some Other Women, for whom I was briefly sad.

Then yesterday brought grief to me...
Today, in heart, I join your sisterhood.

Editor's note: "Women in Grief" (written at the time this collection was in production) and "Discipline" (theme poem appearing among title pages) are unpaged by editorial choice.

ABOUT THE AUTHOR

After earning a journalism degree in special writing at the University of Missouri-Columbia, Betty Cook Rottmann began a career in public relations for her alma mater. Her various writings and poetry appear in publications throughout the United States. She also is the author of several bio-sketches published in *Show-Me Missouri Women,* and she initiated development of the *Guide to Women's Collections* in the Western Historical Manuscript Collection of the State Historical Society of Missouri.

Rottmann has served as regional vice president of the American Association of University Women and has moderated discussion panels for the International Federation of University Women in the United States, Canada, and Japan.

This collection of poetry stems from Rottmann's experiences as career woman, wife, and mother. Her son Larry, a veteran of the Vietnam War, inspired Cry from the Parapet, a group of mother/son poems about the war. Another section evolved from her experiences in raising a daughter and son.

Betty Cook Rottmann is a communications consultant who lives in Columbia, Missouri.